Tortoises
Through the Lens

A Visual Exploration of a Mojave Desert Icon

Tortoises
Through the Lens

A Visual Exploration of a Mojave Desert Icon

Edited by David Lamfrom and Rana Knighten

Sᴜɴʙᴇʟᴛ Pᴜʙʟɪᴄᴀᴛɪᴏɴꜱ
San Diego, California

Tortoises Through the Lens

Sunbelt Publications, Inc.

Printed in Cooperation with the National Parks Conservation Association

National Parks Conservation Association®
Protecting Our National Parks for Future Generations®

Edited by Jennifer Silva Redmond
Book design and composition by Kathleen Wise
Front cover photograph by Marcus Estevane
Back cover photographs by Joshua Marsden and Lindsay Miller
Printed by Everbest Printing Co. in China through Four Colour Print Group
Printed on sustainable, FSC certified paper:

Mixed Sources
Product group from well-managed
forests, and other controlled sources
www.fsc.org Cert no. SGS-COC-003563
© 1996 Forest Stewardship Council
FSC

Sunbelt Publications
1250 Fayette St.
El Cajon, CA 92020
(619) 258-4911, fax: (619) 258-4916
www.sunbeltbooks.com
mail@sunbeltpub.com

14 13 12 11 10   5 4 3 2 1

Library of Congress Cataloging-in-Publication Data

Tortoises through the lens : a visual exploration of a Mojave Desert icon / edited by David Lamfrom and Rana Knighten.
    p. cm.
  ISBN 978-0-916251-01-7
  1. Desert tortoise. 2. Endangered species. I. Lamfrom, David. II. Knighten, Rana.
  QL666.C584T47 2010
  597.92'4--dc22
              2010018415

Sponsors

RICHARD AND RHODA

GOLDMAN

FUND

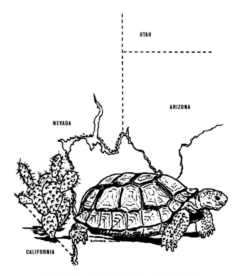

DESERT TORTOISE COUNCIL

Contents

Acknowledgements

This project would not exist without support, funding, advice, and dedicated effort from innumerable individuals and organizations. We greatly appreciate Audubon Society/ Toyota Motor Company's collaborative TogetherGreen program for recognizing the value of our idea and for giving us the initial grant, training, and inspiration to bring this concept to reality. We give special thanks to the entire TogetherGreen team, who provided leadership and vision to this project. National Parks Conservation Association has been supportive of this project since its inception and was an essential force behind all of our efforts. Numerous individuals in the organization, such as Michael Cipra, Ron Sundergill, and Seth Shteir gave willingly of their time and talents to push our work forward, and to help us create the best possible program. We extend special thanks to Mojave National Preserve who has been a steady partner throughout this process, providing us a meeting space for education, giving their time, and allowing us to show our artwork in their Desert Light Gallery. Mojave National Preserve employees Linda Slater, Dennis Schramm, Debra Hughson, and Neal Darby — your time and guidance are appreciated. Thank you to the Goldman Foundation for their crucial support, which provided us the opportunity to expand the program to educate youth on climate change in the desert and beyond. Thanks to the Mojave Environmental Education Consortium for embracing our idea and helping us to recruit students, and then connect them to the Mojave Desert. The Desert Tortoise Council, a group that works tirelessly to protect the desert tortoise and its habitat, was kind enough to fund, review, and edit our work. Special thanks to Kit McGinnis and the National Park Trust for funding field trips and providing opportunities for our students to form deep connections with our National Parks. The introduction of NPT's Buddy Bison was a special benefit on our travels, and the students created games and fun activities, ranging from brilliant to downright strange, based on Buddy's presence. The San Diego Zoo and the lovely Paula Kahn and her staff at the Desert Tortoise Conservation Center were kind enough to educate our group and to encourage us to give back by welcoming us to their facility for a day of work. Paula is an inspiration to us all and we appreciate the hard work her team does every day to protect desert tortoises. We were lucky to have talented professional photographers such as Josh Schachter and Michael Gordon working with us; thank you for helping our students to express their talents and their unique viewpoints. Thanks to Jane Cipra, for finding tortoises for us, and inspiring our students — especially our female students, who learned that careers in wildlife biology and natural sciences are not only for men. Importantly, praise and respect is due to the parents and families of our thirteen students. Your enduring support, and your thoughtful and gifted children made this project a success, and that is a direct reflection on you.

We would also like to thank individuals like Lisa Belenky, Eric Clough, and groups such as the Southwestern Herpetological Society, and the California Turtle and Tortoise Club of Chino and Long Beach for support, information, recruitment, and donations. Thanks to Hanna Strauss who helped this project in its infancy by finding us opportunities to speak, helping recruit students, and nominating our project for the Jarchow Conservation Award. Thanks to Garry George for his time, and his willingness to provide education to our students. Finally, we would like to honor all those who have persevered through tough political fights, continually shrinking tortoise habitats, and the pain of seeing so much lost, to continue to fight for science-based conservation for the desert tortoise. This charismatic reptile is unique in the entire world, and is our Mojave desert icon to honor or sacrifice.

Our ancestors viewed the earth as rich and bountiful, which it is. Many people in the past also saw nature as inexhaustibly sustainable, which we know is the case only if we care for it. It is not difficult to forgive destruction in the past that resulted from ignorance. Today, however, we have access to more information, and it is essential that we re-examine ethically what we have inherited, what we are responsible for, and what we will pass on to coming generations.

— HIS HOLINESS THE 14TH DALAI LAMA OF TIBET

Foreword

For many years, it was common for people who visited the wild California desert to grab a tortoise as a souvenir. Desert tortoises are charismatic animals. The hatchlings are unbelievably cute. And the species was once so abundant that residents in Joshua Tree, California, used to collect wild tortoises the first weekend each May, paint their shells, and set them to race against each other. Punctuated by generous amounts of beer, this festival was called "Turtle Days," and was used as a marketing tool to entice visitors to the desert.

Nobody spent too much time considering the impact of this treatment on tortoises until the animals started disappearing from the wild. A virulent respiratory disease decimated the tortoise population in the 1970s and 1980s. The juvenile tortoise's most ravenous predator, the raven, has increased its population a thousand-fold with the growth of human communities and the food trash we leave uncovered. Large-scale development in the desert also meant the destruction and fragmentation of tortoise habitat.

Desert tortoise populations in some areas declined by as much as 90% during the 1980s, and the Mojave population is currently listed as threatened by the U.S. Fish and Wildlife Service, meaning it is illegal to collect or harm tortoises.

This species, once so plentiful that visitors to Joshua Tree could witness thousands of hatchlings running across roads, is now on the brink of extinction in the wild.

We are handing our children a world with serious environmental challenges. Climate change, air pollution, deforestation, loss of species… it is easy to look at this daunting list and become discouraged.

The first lesson our children must learn is how to see and share the wonder of the natural world. The antidote for despair is watching a desert tortoise chew on wildflowers until his mouth is smeared with green lipstick from the plant's juices. And with the knowledge of what faces this animal, it is an act of true hopefulness and courage to take a photograph of this scene and share it with others. To say to our friends, our family, our teachers, our elected officials, "This is what I've witnessed. This is what is worth protecting."

The book you hold in your hands is empowering. It represents the wonder and courage and emerging artistic skills of students from diverse California desert communities as they have learned about the threatened animal who is their neighbor, met that neighbor face-to-face in the wild, and stepped forward to share their experience.

This two-year journey started in 2008 when conservationists David Lamfrom and Rana Knighten hatched this visionary plan. David and Rana grew up in inner-city Florida, and they found the natural world through the amphibians and reptiles that spilled out of the Everglades and Big Cypress into the edges of their urban world. David and Rana discovered each other, and the intersection of love, the desire to learn about and protect the Earth, and a mutual interest in strange reptilian creatures drew them to the Mojave Desert. Reflecting on their own path, they wanted to create an opportunity for others. So they found grants, and they willed *Tortoises Through the Lens* into existence. Every weekend in the spring of 2009, David and Rana led their group of students on field trips in the California desert. They hired and recruited experts to provide the students training in wildlife photography, ecology, and conservation. And then they did the most important thing—they empowered the students to find their own vision and voice, and got out of the way.

This multi-faceted book is a product of love, diverse perspectives, and profound faith in the future survival of a species. Look at the images in the pages that follow and think about it: This is what the next generation, our children, want us to see.

— Michael Cipra

Introduction

Tortoises Through the Lens is a community-based action project created to provide thirteen California desert high school students with an opportunity to explore and experience the Mojave Desert. The project uses photography to tell the story of the Mojave's threatened desert tortoise through the eyes of the students. Each student was given a camera, was provided education and training, and was guided to beautiful Mojave Desert landscapes in order to photograph tortoises, wildflowers, landscapes, and each other. The intention of the project is to allow the students to develop a personal and profound relationship with the landscape and the creatures that inhabit it, and to empower the students to communicate the value of this land through their photography. We believe that these transformative personal experiences will benefit them throughout their lives.

Each of the students brings a diverse set of experiences, interests, and talents to the table, so they were given the space to work together in developing the backbone of the project. After much discussion, they decided on the subject matter of the book, opted to give back by volunteering a day of service at the Desert Tortoise Conservation Center, and spent extra time sorting photos for inclusion in this book. Each student sacrificed Saturdays—and occasionally Sundays—to learn, explore, teach, camp, and create beautiful art.

Over the course of many months, in iconic locations such as Mojave National Preserve and Joshua Tree National Park, thousands of photographs were taken. Many of those photos are included in this book, including work from each of the project's participants. Additionally, student photos from this project have been used to illustrate news articles, magazine articles, and newsletters. The student artists will be featured in gallery exhibits, with proceeds from prints or book sales being infused into tortoise conservation efforts of the students' choosing.

The students not only learned about tortoises and the Mojave Desert, they developed a stewardship ethic based on their experiences. The students worked together, despite great differences, to produce a compelling story of why tortoises are worth preserving, and why the desert should be considered more than a racetrack between great cities. The students honed their own creative voices through photography and discussion, and are using this platform to demonstrate their world-view. Through outreach efforts, more than 1 million individuals will be able to consider their message.

Some members of my generation, and older generations, have a mistaken belief that students would rather play video games than hike a desert wash. This is an issue of relevance as well as accessibility—how do you access opportunities you don't know exist, or haven't experienced? I was not surprised by the student's engagement with nature, or their spirit of exploration. I was however, humbled by their genuineness, creativity, and connection to places they had only read about prior to the project. Seeing them experience their first tortoise in the wild reminded me of seeing mine. Watching them embrace their first sequoia, or wander the sinuous Banshee Canyon reminded me of the responsibility we have to share our natural world with them.

— David Lamfrom

CHAPTER 1: | *The Toughest Tortoise*

Tortoises have been a part of North American landscapes for 50 million years or longer. The desert tortoise (*Gopherus agassizii*) has existed for roughly 18 million years relatively unchanged, pre-dating the formation of major North American deserts.

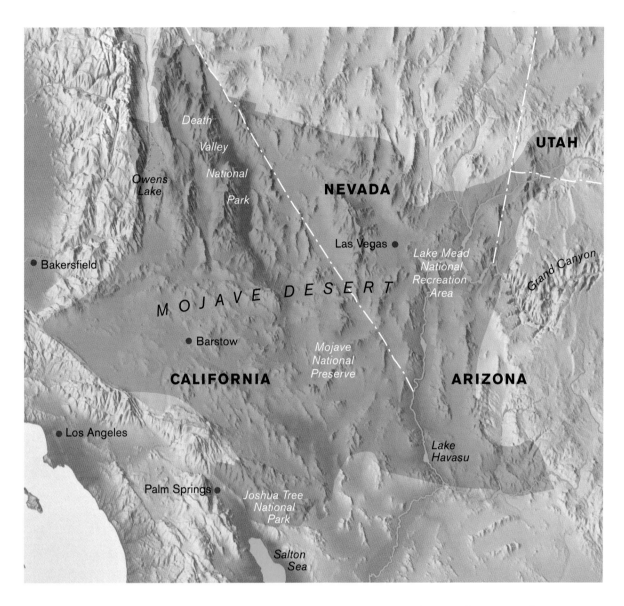

Roughly 15 thousand years ago, during the last North American Ice Age, the area that is now the Mojave Desert was much cooler and wetter. Tortoises shared the land with prehistoric animals such as the mammoth and saber-toothed cats. When the Ice Age ended, the landscape became much dryer and hotter, eventually becoming desert. Today, the Mojave Desert is the smallest and driest of the four North American deserts. It extends from Southwestern Utah to Southeastern California and into Northwestern Arizona. The Mojave population of desert tortoises lives throughout this range west of the Colorado River.

The Mojave population of desert tortoises is distinct from other populations. They have thrived in the extreme conditions of the Mojave by adopting physical and behavioral strategies to take advantage of the short seasons of available food and water. These adaptations allow them to live in many different Mojave ecosystems.

Tortoises have shared this land with human beings for many thousands of years. Throughout this history, people have had many different relationships with tortoises. Some Native American tribes used tortoises as a food source, while others considered tortoises sacred and would not eat them. Some tribes used tortoise shells and other body parts for ceremonial objects, including rattles. At least one tribe referred to the tortoise as "old iron clothes," referring to its tough covering.

The Mojave contains some peaks over 10,000 feet tall, as well as the lowest elevation point in the western hemisphere at 282 feet below sea level, and some of the hottest temperatures and driest conditions on Earth. Despite these harsh conditions, the Mojave Desert teems with life. A highly diverse desert, it contains roughly 2,600 species of plants, 25% of which are found nowhere else on earth. The Mojave is also home to living soils known as cryptobiotic crusts, and an array of wildlife including roadrunner, quail, golden eagle, red-tailed hawk, coyote, badger, mountain lion, desert bighorn sheep, several species of rattlesnakes, chuckwalla, Gila monster, and the desert tortoise.

The Mojave Desert, the smallest and driest desert in North America, is a land of mountains and valleys. It is characterized by brutally hot summers, near-freezing winters, and strong winds. In an average year, much of the Mojave receives less than 5 inches of precipitation, with the majority falling in the winter. With well-timed winter rains, spring in the Mojave is a spectacular sight. Annual wildflowers carpet the usually sparse desert floor, providing food and moisture for desert wildlife.

Cacti are an essential part of the ecosystem and are found in most Mojave Desert habitats. Cacti are succulents, able to store water in their leaves and stems. Many species of wildlife eat the cactus fruits, flowers, and stems for food and to obtain their stored moisture. Cacti also provide shelter and shade for a host of Mojave species.

Biological soil crusts are an important part of the Mojave Desert. These cryptobiotic crusts consist of cyanobacteria, lichens, and mosses, which form a mat of filaments. This mat creates a protective crust over the naturally thin and sandy desert soil, helping to keep in moisture, reducing erosion, and trapping seeds. Cryptobiotic crusts also stabilize the soil and help other desert plants to obtain vital nutrients. Without soil crusts, vegetation that is essential for the survival of desert wildlife would find it difficult to gain a foothold in the arid Mojave.

*The desert tortoise shares its habitat with many different animals,
all of which have adapted to thrive in the Mojave's harsh conditions.*

Bighorn sheep inhabit steep, rocky slopes and feed on grasses and other plants. They use their superb climbing abilities to evade predators such as the mountain lion.

Many lizards call the Mojave Desert home. This horned lizard feeds almost exclusively on harvester ants, while more aggressive species — such as leopard lizards — consume a wide variety of prey, including other lizards. Female leopard lizards exhibit bright orange splotches during the breeding season.

Coyotes are one of the top predators in the Mojave Desert and have a varied diet which includes other mammals, birds, eggs, reptiles, plants and fruits, and carrion. Coyotes are one of the few natural predators of adult desert tortoises.

Scorpions, common arachnids of the Mojave Desert, live in underground burrows or other shelters during the day and emerge at night to find food and mates.

The desert tortoise has found ways to live in diverse habitats in the Mojave Desert.

Creosote bushes are adaptable to many environmental conditions, making them a dominant low-elevation Mojave plant species. Creosote Bush Scrub is often associated with loose soils, making it a perfect habitat for burrowing species.

Pinyon-Juniper Woodland is encountered above 4,500 feet in the Mojave Desert. This plant community is cooler and wetter than lower elevation habitats. Pine nuts and juniper berries provide energy-rich food sources for many species.

Joshua-Tree Woodland is dominated by the iconic Joshua Tree. This diverse desert ecosystem is anchored by a complex web of plant and animal interactions largely centered around the life cycle of the Joshua Tree. Even fallen Joshua Trees provide homes for small mammals, lizards, and insects.

The Mojave contains several of the most impressive and extensive dune systems in North America. These sand mountains and their surrounding areas provide habitat for plants and animals that are specially adapted to live in this ecosystem. Species such as the kit fox, Mojave fringe-toed lizard, and sidewinder rattlesnake all have specialized anatomical features for life on the dunes.

Desert tortoises have evolved some interesting adaptations to survive the Mojave Desert's scant precipitation and high rate of evaporation. They dig burrows, some over 20 feet in length, helping them to escape extreme heat, cold, and wind. In addition to nightly shelter, tortoises also use their burrows to hibernate for extended periods during the winter and estivate during the hottest part of the summer. Hibernation and estivation allow their metabolism to slow until food and water resources become available.

Unlike the other warm North American deserts (Sonoran and Chihuahuan), the Mojave receives almost all of its precipitation during the winter months. Desert tortoises are well adapted to take advantage of the precious seasonal moisture. Their bladder can hold up to 40% of their body weight in water for future use. Amazingly, this stored water can sustain them for a year or more. This is a valuable adaptation in an environment prone to drought.

Tortoises consume most of their food in spring, in the form of moisture-rich annual plants. The amount and timing of precipitation determines when these plants bloom and seed. In a good spring, desert blooms are abundant, providing an important source of food and water for desert tortoises.

All turtles and tortoises have shells. Damage to the shell can be life-threatening because the backbone is fused to the roof of the shell. The shell is living, and continues to grow throughout their lives. The upper part of the shell is known as the carapace, while the bottom is the plastron. The plates of the shell are termed scutes and each scute develops growth rings throughout a turtle or tortoise's lifetime. Damage to scutes can harm or disfigure a turtle or tortoise.

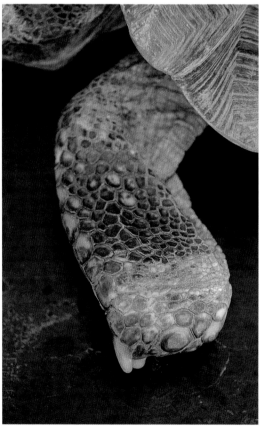

Desert tortoises have sturdy elephantine limbs, ending in large claws. These are the perfect tools to dig burrows and navigate the spiny desert landscape.

Tortoises are vegetarians, eating an amazing array of fruits, flowers, and leaves of annual wildflowers and grasses. The evidence of what a tortoise eats is often worn on the tortoise's face like a green or red lipstick.

Desert tortoises are both architects and gardeners—shaping the Mojave ecosystem. They dig burrows that provide habitat for themselves and other species. They also excavate basins that collect precious rainwater and they distribute seeds of fruit, grass, and other vegetation by passing them through their digestive tract across the landscape.

A female tortoise can store sperm for 5 years or longer, ensuring she can bring forth the next generation whether or not she finds a mate that year.

Desert tortoises engage in many territorial, defensive, and breeding behaviors. Male tortoises will fight by using a bony horn on the front of their plastron, called a gular horn, to try to flip their opponent. Breeding behavior is similarly violent, as males will head-bob, bite the female's legs, or ram the female's shells with their gular horns in hopes of successfully mating.

Female desert tortoises lay a clutch of between 6–12 eggs. Desert tortoises in the Mojave generally have smaller clutches of 4–8 eggs, but they are able to nest up to three times per year, when food and moisture are plentiful.

Desert tortoises are the size of a silver dollar at birth, and are born with soft, flexible shells. It may take four or more years for a desert tortoise's shell to harden enough to protect it from predators. During this time, they are extremely vulnerable and can be eaten by most Mojave predators. Adult tortoises have few natural predators.

CHAPTER 2: | *Threats to a Mojave Icon*

Hundreds of thousands of desert tortoises are currently kept in captivity, mainly in the desert southwest. They are sought after as pets due to their personality, curiosity, and longevity. Collection of desert tortoises from the wild is a significant threat to the survival of this species.

It is unlawful to touch, take, harm, or harass a desert tortoise in the wild unless it is in imminent danger. If a tortoise is along a busy road and must be moved, carefully help it across the road carrying it low to the ground and walking slowly. Place it out of harm's way, and facing the direction it was already going. Remember to handle the tortoise as little as possible because it may respond to stress by urinating, a defense mechanism to repel predators. Causing a tortoise to void its stored water may leave the tortoise without enough water to survive until the next rain.

Many owners of captive tortoises allow or encourage their tortoises to breed. A successful nest can result in many baby desert tortoises that cannot be released into the wild and cannot be given away as pets. These tortoises may live 80 or more years and can quickly become a burden on owners who cannot provide the proper diet and outdoor homes for them.

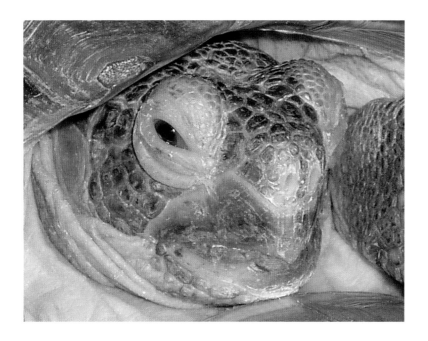

Desert tortoises must live outdoors, regardless of their size or age. There is no lightbulb or heat lamp in the world that can provide the exact heat and light requirements necessary for a desert tortoise. If not provided with natural heat and sunlight and not allowed to thermoregulate naturally, it will not be able to digest its food properly. The undigested food will rot away in a tortoise's stomach, causing the tortoise to become septic. Under these conditions, a tortoise will not be able to absorb necessary nutrients and its body will begin to extract calcium from its own shell and bones. This combination of conditions will cause the tortoise to slowly decompose from the inside out.

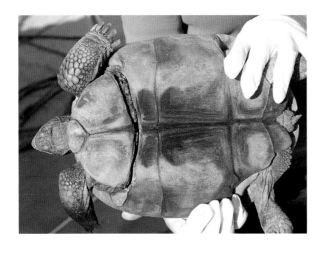

Captive tortoise owners often paint or glue objects to their tortoise's shell. Tortoise shells are made of living tissue. Paint and adhesives can be absorbed through a tortoise's shell and can be toxic to the tortoise and cause permanent damage to its shell.

Returning captive or poached tortoises back to the wild is also detrimental to native tortoise populations. Tortoises that are reintroduced may be carrying Upper Respiratory Tract Disease (URTD) or other infectious pathogens that can spread through wild populations.

Upper Respiratory Tract Disease in desert tortoises is caused by a bacterial (*Mycoplasma spp.*) infection. Similar to a cold, the symptoms can include nasal and ocular discharge, difficulties in breathing, lethargy, and for some tortoises, death. This infection can be common in captive populations. It's important not to release captive tortoises into the wild so that disease-free tortoises do not become infected. These tortoises show symptoms of the disease.

Exposure to Upper Respiratory Tract Disease is not an immediate death sentence for the desert tortoise. Many tortoises have been exposed to URTD but do not develop the disease, and lead long and healthy lives. These tortoises are otherwise healthy and may become a future resource for desert tortoise recovery.

Even if a tortoise does become sick, the bacterium cannot be transmitted from a mother to her eggs, allowing hatchlings to emerge with a clean bill of health.

Desert tortoises have a strong homing instinct, and relocated or released tortoises may try to return to their "home," spending critical water and food stores and risking death. If you have a desert tortoise you no longer can care for, contact a local wildlife agency, a herpetological society, or a turtle and tortoise club. Do not release a captive tortoise into the wild.

Coyotes are one of the few natural predators of the adult desert tortoise. Coyotes generally prey on small mammals like kangaroo rats, packrats, ground squirrels, and rabbits. In years that are especially dry or when prey is scarce, coyotes will switch to available food sources, including desert tortoises.

Coyote populations have increased adjacent to urbanized areas because of the availability of year-round food resources like trash, pet food, and pets themselves. Water is also readily available from sprinklers, golf courses, ponds, and agricultural lands.

Another predator that has benefitted from urbanization is the raven. The population of this cunning problem-solver has grown exponentially due to the availability of food and water along roads and developed areas. Ravens have learned to prey upon juvenile tortoises. This behavior is taught to their offspring, producing generations of ravens that prey on tortoises.

The increased predation on young tortoises decreases the already low survivorship of young tortoises into adulthood, which may be less than 2 percent. This is coupled with the late sexual maturity of Mojave's desert tortoises, which may take 12–20 years to reach breeding age. Raven predation is a major threat to desert tortoise populations, preventing them from recruiting breeding-age adults, thus reducing the number of eggs produced.

Habitat loss and habitat fragmentation are significant threats to desert tortoise populations. Urban areas like Las Vegas, Pahrump, the Antelope Valley, Victor Valley, Morongo Basin, and parts of the Coachella Valley were all prime tortoise habitats, prior to development. Habitat fragmentation results in barriers to food and water resources that tortoises are unable to cross. Also, populations on either side of these barriers are isolated and no longer able to share their genes. This is destructive to the overall health of the species.

The proximity of development to tortoise habitats attracts other threats as well, including a higher density of predators such as pet and feral dogs, coyotes, and ravens. Human development also increases the presence of invasive plants which outcompete native species, robbing tortoises of their preferred food sources. The number of roads and off-road trails through tortoise habitat increases with development, as does the tortoise mortality from on- and off-road vehicles.

Tortoises are susceptible to being run over for many reasons. They move slowly, look like rocks on the road, eat roadside vegetation, and retract into their shells when frightened. Sandy soils used by tortoises are also favored locations for off-road vehicle recreation, bringing these vehicles and tortoises into conflict. Care must be taken to avoid crushing tortoises, their burrows, and the vegetation necessary for their survival. Recreationists, such as hikers and off-road vehicle users, should be careful to avoid damaging desert pavement, which protects the desert soils and vegetation.

Tortoises often find shade beneath parked vehicles. When you're in tortoise habitat, always check under your vehicle before you leave.

In the Mojave Desert, a land of extreme temperatures and scarce water, species have adopted specific strategies to survive. Changing climate patterns could upset this precarious balance and desert inhabitants may not be able to change quickly enough to persist.

If global warming and climate change remain unchecked, summer temperatures in the desert may be higher and harsh seasons may last longer. Rainfall will be less predictable and conditions may become more favorable for the colonization of invasive plants and animals, displacing Mojave natives. Will conditions change the essential character of the Mojave? Are we dooming species that have adapted specialized relationships to the Mojave's climate patterns and ecosystems?

The desert tortoise is facing a host of threats, many of which work synergistically. Populations of wily predators like ravens and coyotes will continue to grow if we do not stop providing easy food sources like trash and dog food. Invasive plants will continue to colonize critical tortoise habitat and reduce nutrient-dense food supplies if we do not limit our pollution, and do not actively remove invasives from our public lands. Reduced food quality will impair tortoise's immune systems and make them more vulnerable to diseases like URTD. We will continue to lose tortoises on roads, and in habitat, if we cannot responsibly recreate in their habitat.

When in desert tortoise country, we must drive at careful speeds to avoid hitting tortoises. When driving off-road, we must avoid destroying tortoise burrows, and tortoise burrow aprons (area in front of burrows where eggs are usually laid). With populations of the desert tortoise declining throughout the Mojave, we need to change the way we think about the value of the desert and improve our collective behavior in order to save this imperiled species.

CHAPTER 3: | *Tortoises Tomorrow?*

In 1990, the U.S. Fish and Wildlife Service listed the Mojave population of the desert tortoise under the federal Endangered Species Act as a "threatened" species. Under the terms of the California Endangered Species Act, the California Fish and Game Commission also listed the desert tortoise as "threatened" in 1989. These listings were based on solid evidence of local population declines in much of the Mojave Desert due to habitat loss and degradation (the result of livestock overgrazing, off-road vehicle activity, urbanization, agricultural development, etc.), significant predation by ravens and coyotes, and Upper Respiratory Tract Disease. The listings demonstrate our awareness that, without corrective actions, the Mojave desert tortoise will become "Endangered." As part of the federal listing of the tortoise, a recovery plan was issued in 1994, and revised in 2010. The purpose of this plan is to recover the species to a point where the population is sustainable and listing is no longer required.

Tortoises once thrived in the Mojave Desert. Without question, the changes to tortoise habitat are directly attributable to human activities. Unlike many species of plants and animals that have already gone extinct, we can still save the desert tortoise. Our actions today can ensure that those who follow us have the joy of encountering one of these amazing creatures in their native habitat, not just in a zoo or backyard.

Current conservation efforts:

Interest groups, non-profit organizations and government agencies have invested significant time, research, and funding to help recover the desert tortoise. Military bases that have large tracts of land in the Mojave Desert have instituted desert tortoise head start programs. These programs provide enclosures for young tortoises to allow them critical time for their shells to harden prior to release. Joshua Tree National Park has installed barriers along its road system to decrease tortoise road mortality. Joshua Tree National Park is also conducting research on the range and seasonal dispersal of desert tortoises within the park. The Desert Tortoise Recovery Office of the U.S. Fish and Wildlife Service focuses on coordinating research and recovery efforts among non-governmental organizations and state and federal agencies. The Desert Tortoise Council promotes tortoise conservation through annual symposia, bringing together academics, agency representatives, and interested citizens to discuss threats to desert tortoises, and by education, raising awareness, and promoting desert tortoise research.

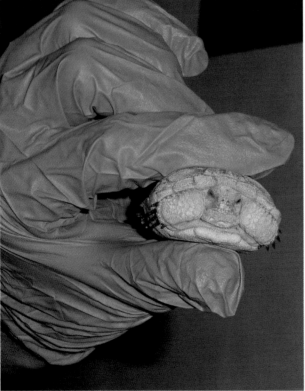

The Desert Tortoise Natural Area was established in 1974 as the first tortoise preserve in the Southwestern United States. This nearly 40 square mile area is managed by the Bureau of Land Management and the Desert Tortoise Preserve Committee. The management protects the habitat and provides a naturalist to guide visitors and school groups on hikes through the preserve, educating them about tortoises and the Western Mojave Desert ecosystem. The site features interpretative displays and materials that teach about tortoise biology, ecology, and threats.

In March 2009, the San Diego Zoo's Institute for Conservation Research began administering the Desert Tortoise Conservation Center in Las Vegas, Nevada. The main goal of the center is the conservation of the Mojave Desert ecosystem, including recovery of the desert tortoise. The center accepts unwanted captive or injured tortoises through the southern Nevada Desert Tortoise Hotline. They receive more than 1000 desert tortoises every year. Most of these are unwanted pets, many of which did not receive proper care and require rehabilitation. These tortoises live at the center indefinitely. In all, the center cares for approximately 3000 desert tortoises, which requires significant time and resources. Routine tortoise care at the facility includes conducting medical tests, providing treatment for illness or injury, and performing surgical procedures when necessary.

In the Las Vegas Valley, thousands of desert tortoises are kept as pets and bred while wild populations are diminishing. The San Diego Zoo and its partners are working to shape the facility as one that will support tortoise recovery efforts. They are accomplishing this through on-the-ground recovery actions, as well as conducting research, training biologists, and educating the public.

The Mojave National Preserve in southeastern California will be opening its new LEED Certified Desert Tortoise Research Center in late 2010. This facility will host research on the survival of juvenile desert tortoises and the potential to augment populations through tortoise head start programs. State of the art exclosures, which are designed to keep predators out, rather than to keep tortoises in, will protect juveniles until they are large enough to resist predation by ravens. Field work over several years has shown a significant impact of roads on tortoise populations. The Preserve is seeking funding to install barrier fencing along roads, improve driver awareness, and increase law enforcement efforts.

Land managers must carefully consider how management policies affect tortoises. Decision makers must consider options such as installing fencing along roads and working to eradicate invasive plant species in prime tortoise habitat. As time goes on, it will become increasingly important to protect tortoise habitat and to connect these protected areas. This is vital to allow tortoises from different areas to mate and to spread the new genetic material necessary for healthy populations. Connectivity of protected lands also allows tortoises to expand their range when resources are scarce, giving them a better chance of survival in the face of changing conditions due to global climate change.

Small-scale efforts are key in tortoise conservation. Municipalities, businesses, travelers, and homeowners can reduce the unnatural numbers of predatory ravens and coyotes by making trash and other potential food sources less readily available. A commitment to reducing waste and responsibly storing and covering our trash benefits us all. Such measures will reduce costs, save space in landfills, and ensure that garbage does not litter our desert.

Individuals can play a huge part in the recovery of the desert tortoise. We can help tortoises and their habitat by:

— not littering or illegally dumping in the desert,

— not removing tortoises from the wild,

— not returning captive tortoises to the wild,

— not breeding desert tortoises in captivity,

— not touching or harassing tortoises,

— staying on established hiking and OHV trails in tortoise habitat,

— driving aware and at reasonable speeds in tortoise habitat,

— and by educating others about the value of tortoises and how to protect them.

Protecting tortoise habitat benefits all plants and animals in the Mojave Desert ecosystem, including humans. Protected lands are a living laboratory for students and our children to learn about our world. These lands provide enjoyment for individuals and produce jobs and tourism for desert communities. Our desert is a national treasure, drawing visitors from around the world who seek the solitude, beauty, starry night skies, and abundant wildlife and wildflowers of the Mojave.

Attitudes are changing, and will continue to change. As more and more people recreate in the desert and help stimulate local economies, more people will care for this natural wonder. This new attitude and support will help to protect iconic and threatened species, like the desert tortoise, so that those who follow us will know the privilege of walking in a desert with its natural legacy intact.

The ultimate fate of the desert tortoise rests in our hands. If the tortoise is to survive, we must reconsider how we value our desert and what we will do to protect it. Those who have spent time in these rugged and scenic landscapes understand that there is no place quite like the Mojave Desert. This desert, complete with tortoises and bighorn sheep, wildflowers, caves, and pine-covered mountains, is one of the last true wide-open spaces remaining.

Student Participants

Amy Bailey

Amy Bailey was selected as a participant in the Tortoises Through the Lens program and contributed to this photobook.

Lucas Basulto

"Wildlife conservation and photography have always been huge passions in my life, so I am extremely happy that I got the chance to combine the two in order to help these tortoises in the struggles that they face."

Keya Cason

"Photography, for me, is a way to give the world a new perspective on things, but with my adventures with Tortoise Through the Lens, *I gained something; I gained a new appreciation for the desert."*

Marcus Estavane

*"*Tortoises Through the Lens *has been a fun project for me. I've learned so much from the meetings and trips we have had, it is definitely an experience I will never forget, and would love to do again."*

Jackson Shane Gallant

"I've always liked reptiles and photography. Combining the two allows me to 'capture the animals and bring them home' without removing them from nature. With the Tortoises Through the Lens *project, I can bring these amazing creatures into the homes of others as well."*

Krista Hoffman

"It has been an awesome experience to be involved in the making of this book. I learned a lot and I hope it makes people more aware of how fragile the future of the Desert Tortoise is."

Joshua Marsden

"Participating in the Tortoises Through the Lens *program has taught me a lot about nature and its inhabitants. I have learned what I can do to help conserve what is being lost."*

Kaitlyn Medley

"Complaining about your life is just wasting it away; do something and make a difference!"

Lindsay Miller

"Where words and voices fail, art speaks."

Wyatt Myers

"Every time I heard about a field trip, I got really excited, because I never knew what new experience and adventures that we would have. On every field trip we would find something that I had never seen before."

Lea Paige

"This was a great experience. I knew a lot already, but 'through the lens' I seemed to learn so much more. I had fun and it was a great time to learn and experience."

Dakota Sprout

*"*Tortoises Through the Lens *really inspired me to learn more about the desert. The field trips we took made me think of the desert differently; it used to be boring to me and now I see life everywhere. I can't wait to go back and continue my work with the desert tortoise."*

Rachel Wilson

*"*Tortoises Through the Lens—*it's not just a photography class, but a movement to change the continuous struggle that tortoises must go through because of human interference."*

Student Photo Index

Additional photos were provided by:
Daniel Essary, Rachel Foster, Paula Kahn,
Rana Knighten, David Lamfrom, and Isaac Rivadeneira

David Lamfrom, a Mojave Desert-based Field Representative for the National
Parks Conservation Association, works to protect National Parks and Preserves,
wildlands, and wildlife in the California desert. David hopes to inspire the next
generation, through photography and direct exposure, to steward the remarkable
resources of the Mojave, and to inspire leaders and communities to honor,
preserve and protect these places on behalf of those who will inherit them.

Rana Knighten lives and works in southern California's Mojave Desert.
She is an interpretative Park Ranger at Mojave National Preserve, and a
nature and wildlife photographer. Rana strives to empower youth and
women to deepen their connections to the natural world, and to use
their artistic vision and perception to tell its story.

Resources

The *Tortoises Through the Lens* Photobook is intended to be a photo-based exploration of the Mojave desert tortoise. It is not intended to be a primary reference, and it is not a purely scientific look at the subject matter. That being said, extensive research was conducted to verify the accuracy of the book's text. The text was reviewed by the Desert Tortoise Council to ensure responsible and accurate messaging. We drew our research from a handful of resources, which are listed below. Thank you to those researchers, scientists, and naturalists that have spent their careers learning about the Mojave and its inhabitants, in order to help us all understand and protect them. I would also like to honor Kristin Berry, Jeff Lovich, Michael Conner, Paula Kahn and the Desert Tortoise Conservation Center of the San Diego Zoo, Debra Hughson, Jane Cipra, and Ileene Anderson, all of which communicated directly with us to provide insight into the biology, ecology, and conservation of the desert tortoise.

Turtles of the United States and Canada, by Ernst, Barbour, and Lovich, Smithsonian Institution, 1994.

The Sonoran Desert Tortoise—Natural History, Biology, and Conservation, edited by Thomas Van Devender, University of Arizona Press and Arizona-Sonora Desert Museum, 2002.

The Mojave Desert: Ecosystem Processes and Sustainability, edited by Robert H. Webb, Lynn F. Fenstermaker, Jill S. Heaton, Debra L. Hughson, Eric V. McDonald, David M. Miller, University of Nevada Prests, Reno NV, 2009.

www.deserttortoise.org

www.tortoise-tracks.org

http://climate.nasa.gov

http://www.noaa.gov/climate.html

SUNBELT'S SOUTHERN CALIFORNIA BOOKSHELF

Anza-Borrego: A Photographic Journey	Ernie Cowan
Anza-Borrego A to Z: People, Places, and Things	Diana Lindsay
Anza-Borrego Desert Region (Wilderness Press)	L. and D. Lindsay
California Desert Miracle: The Fight for Parks and Wilderness	Frank Wheat
Cycling Los Angeles	D. and S. Brundige
Cycling Orange County	D. and S. Brundige
Cycling the Palm Springs Region	Nelson Copp
Cycling San Diego	Copp, Schad
The Cuyamacas: The Story of San Diego's High Country	Leland Fetzer
Desert Lore of Southern California	Choral Pepper
Earth Pigments and Paint of the California Indians: Meaning and Technology	Paul Douglas Campbell
Fire, Chaparral, and Survival in Southern California	Richard W. Halsey
Fossil Treasures of the Anza-Borrego Desert	Jefferson, Lindsay
Geology of Anza-Borrego: Edge of Creation	Remeika, Lindsay
Marshal South and the Ghost Mountain Chronicles	Diana Lindsay
Mexican Slang Plus Graffiti	Linton Robinson
Mining History and Geology of Joshua Tree (SDAG)	Margaret Eggers, ed.
Palm Springs Legends: Creation of a Desert Oasis	Greg Niemann
Palm Springs Oasis: A Photographic Essay	Greg Lawson
Palm Springs-Style Gardening	Maureen Gilmer
Peaks, Palms, and Picnics: Day Journeys in The Coachella Valley	Linda Pyle
Spanish Lingo for the Savvy Gringo	Elizabeth Reid
Strangers in a Stolen Land: History of Indians in San Diego County	Richard Carrico
This Day in California History	Carl Palm

Incorporated in 1988, with roots in publishing since 1973, Sunbelt Publications produces and distributes natural science and outdoor guidebooks, regional histories and pictorials, and stories that celebrate the land and its people.

Sunbelt books help to discover and conserve the natural, historical, and cultural heritage of unique regions on the frontiers of adventure and learning. Our books guide readers into distinctive communities and special places, both natural and man-made.

We carry hundreds of books on southern California!

Visit us online at:

www.sunbeltbooks.com